ESSENTIAL **DK** COMPUTERS

INTERNET

BUYING & SELLING ONLINE

ABOUT THIS BOOK

Buying & Selling Online introduces the largest revolution in retailing since the first department store was opened. The principal difference is that this store covers the planet.

THESE ARE STILL VERY EARLY DAYS IN the history of the world wide web as a tool for ecommerce. Online stores are opening, burgeoning, then folding on a daily basis; hackers, viruses, and web scammers lurk around every corner. These could well be the gold-rush days of '49 except for the difference in the technology. A global revolution is taking place, and, as with all revolutions, the outcome is unpredictable, but things will certainly never be the same again. The real consequences will begin to emerge as the dust slowly settles.

While we're waiting for that to happen, this book attempts to guide you through the battle-scarred highways by showing you how to buy online, make sure your transactions are safe, and take advantage of the bargains appearing on the new auction sites; it also explains how to take the plunge yourself and start selling

online. The book closes with an index of some of the many shopping websites.

The chapters and the subsections present the information principally by using step-by-step sequences. Virtually every step is accompanied by an illustration to show you what you can expect to see onscreen at each stage.

The book contains several features to help you understand both what is happening and what you need to do.

Cross-references are shown in the text as left- or right-hand page icons: ⌐ and ⌐. The page number and the reference are shown at the foot of the page. In addition to the sections of sequential screen shots, there are boxes that explain a feature in detail, and tip boxes that provide further information and alternative methods. Finally, at the back, you will find a glossary of common terms and a comprehensive index to the book.

ESSENTIAL COMPUTERS

INTERNET

BUYING &
SELLING ONLINE

JOHN WATSON

LONDON, NEW YORK, SYDNEY, DELHI, PARIS, MUNICH, and JOHANNESBURG

SENIOR EDITOR Amy Corzine
SENIOR ART EDITOR Sarah Cowley
US EDITORS Gary Werner and Margaret Parrish
DTP DESIGNER Julian Dams
PRODUCTION CONTROLLER Michelle Thomas

MANAGING EDITOR Adèle Hayward
SENIOR MANAGING ART EDITOR Nigel Duffield

Produced for Dorling Kindersley Limited by
Design Revolution Limited, Queens Park Villa,
30 West Drive, Brighton, England BN2 2GE
EDITORIAL DIRECTOR Ian Whitelaw
SENIOR DESIGNER Andy Ashdown
PROJECT EDITOR Ian Kearey
DESIGNER Paul Bowler

First American Edition, 2001

2 4 6 8 10 9 7 5 3 1

First published in the United States by DK Publishing, Inc.,
95 Madison Avenue, New York, New York 10016

DK Publishing offers special discounts for bulk purchases for sales promotions or
premiums. Specific, large-quantity needs can be met with special editions, including
personalized covers, excerpts of existing guides, and corporate imprints.
For more information, contact Special Markets Department, DK Publishing, Inc.,
95 Madison Avenue, New York, NY 10016 Fax: 800-600-9098.

A Cataloging in Publication record is available from the Library of Congress.

ISBN 0-7894-8025-5

Color reproduced by Colourscan, Singapore
Printed and bound in Italy by Graphicom

See our complete catalog at
www.dk.com

CONTENTS

BUYING ONLINE

The number of online purchases is increasing every day, as
is the number of new online retailing companies. Finding
what you want is mostly about knowing how and where to look.

WHY BUY ON THE INTERNET?

In many ways, the development of online
shopping mirrors the growth of large
department stores at the end of the 19th
century. These stores offered convenience,
choice, availability, and lower prices. And
each one of those elements remains a valid
reason why the majority of purchasers are
attracted to buying online today.

CONVENIENCE

● Websites are open and
available for browsing and
ordering 24 hours a day,
seven days a week, from
any location where you
have internet access, which
makes the internet the
ultimate convenience store.
● Additionally, there are
no parking problems to
contend with; the internet
is climate-free due to the
absence of wind, rain,
snow, or gales to make
shopping difficult; and
there are no crowded stores
or malls to fight your way
through to gain access to
what you want to buy.

CHOICE

● The breadth and depth of items offered for sale online is immense, and is matched only by the number of websites dedicated to particular lines of merchandise.

● The tangible goods that are available online range from airplanes to islands and everything in between – let alone the services that are also offered.

● Private islands, for example, are available to buy or rent from **www.vladi-private-islands.de/home_e.html**.

Your opportunity to buy Troop Island has just gone.

● If it's an airplane you want to buy, either as a first-time buyer or to replace the one you're now ashamed of, try **www.wingsonline.com**.

Still, you could always fly over it in a 2000 Aerocomp AC-6/7.

AVAILABILITY

● Most of us, however, have more modest needs than airplanes or islands, and the budgets to match, and this is where the internet can offer help to the online shopper.

● You are likely to find lower prices than those in regular stores for two main reasons. The first is the sheer number of websites that are available – all of which want your business.

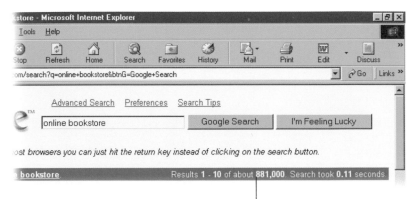

*A search using Google for "**online bookstores**" returned nearly 900,000 hits – many will only be references to them, but many will be actual stores – indicating the competitiveness of the market*

PRICE

● The second reason for lower prices is the presence of price comparison sites, such as **www.bottomdollar. com**, where the prices asked by different retailers for an item of merchandise can be found and compared.

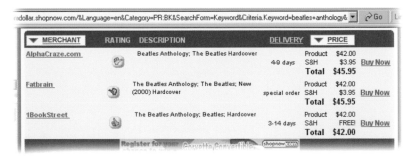

bottomdollar.com *shows that almost $4 can be saved on* The Beatles Anthology *by selective shopping.*

USING A SEARCH ENGINE

A search engine is the most direct way to find what you want to buy. To illustrate how quickly items can be found and purchased, the example here shows how a technical piece of equipment, known as a global positioning system (or GPS) receiver, can be found. A GPS receiver can pinpoint its longitude, latitude, and altitude on the planet to within 20 yards. Many new automobiles are now sold with satellite navigation as standard, and this uses the same technology as a GPS receiver. The buying methods shown here can be applied to any online merchandise.

1 ENTERING THE SEARCH TERM
● The search engine used here is the popular Google; this has the simplest and least cluttered screen of all the major search engines.
● Enter the text, **gps receiver**, into the search field, and then click the **Google Search** button.

2 CHOOSING A WEBSITE
● From the list of hits returned, look for one that appears to include useful advice on selecting a GPS receiver, then select it by clicking on the hotlink.

Retailers will learn that websites that appear helpful to the buyer are more likely to be selected

3 READING THE INFORMATION

● The website selected here – **www.rei.com** – contains a great deal of helpful background information, as well as a highlighted link that you can click on to see their own selection of **GPS Receivers**.

where it can be picked up by any GPS receiver. By measuring how long it takes for these signals to reach it, a GPS receiver can figure out how far away it is from the satellite sending the signal. By performing this task with 3 or more satellites simultaneously, a GPS receiver can determine its exact location through a process called triangulation.

Why are GPS receivers useful?
GPS receivers can tell you exactly where you are anywhere in the world, no matter what the conditions. They work 24 hours a day, 365 days a year, almost anywhere. They work in whiteouts, dense fog, even on the ocean when you have no reference points. Perfomance is hampered only by overhead obstacles like dense tree cover, mountains or buildings that can block satellite signals (and newer models can handle many of these

Shop REI's selection of
GPS Receivers

Highlighted link ●

4 MAKING THE SELECTION

● REI's web page that contains receivers can be sorted by brand or by price. By default, the units are sorted by brand, starting with the range of Garmin receivers.

● The website helpfully says elsewhere that Garmin receivers are the biggest sellers, and that it is best to buy a low-priced model for your first receiver. With that advice, we have clicked on the cheapest model in the Garmin range.

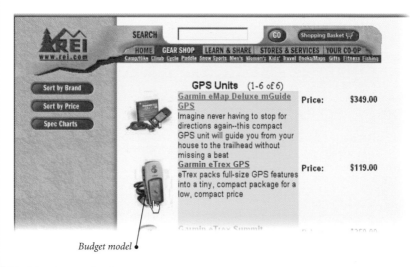

Budget model ●

5 ADDING TO THE BASKET

● The web page for the selected model provides a larger image of the unit and more information about its features.

● If you decide to purchase this particular model, check the options available and click on the **Add to Shopping Basket** button.

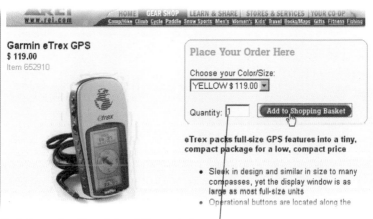

Check the number of items before clicking on the button ●

6 SHOP MORE OR CHECK OUT?

● Having made a selection, the following page usually shows the current contents of the basket and offers you the choice to continue shopping or to proceed to the checkout. A check box is available to remove the item from your basket if you want to change your mind.

● If you don't want to purchase any more items, press the appropriate shipping button in the **Checkout** section.

● All shopping sites contain their own versions of these options, and the icons and buttons naturally will differ.

*All shopping sites have a **Remove** box to check if you change your mind about buying* ●

7 COMPLETING AN ORDER FORM

● The next stage involves completing an order form with your personal details and entering the details of your credit card. You are not committing yourself to anything at this stage because you are not yet sending any information over the internet.

● Once you have completed the order form, most sites ask you to click on a **Continue** button, or otherwise indicate that your order is complete.

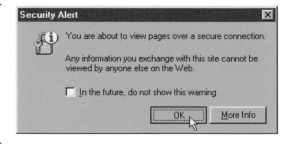

State:	California	(USA only)
Country:	United States	
Postal (Zip) Code:	67432	
Daytime Phone:	1-800-497-6444	
Night Phone/Fax:		(Optional)

5. Shipping Address Same as Billing Address?

- If you want your order shipped to the billing address you entered in Step 4, please check this box and click the "Continue" button.
- In some cases, a signature may be required for delivery of large orders—please have the package sent to an address where someone can sign for it if necessary. A street address is also highly recommended (rather than a PO box), as this makes it easier for us to get your package to you quickly.

☑ Ship my order to my billing address.

CONTINUE

Note: If you want your order shipped to a **different address**, do **NOT** check the box and do **NOT** click "Continue." Instead, fill in the blanks in Step 6.

Done

THE SECURITY ALERT

● When you are about to exchange information across the internet, your web browser displays a security alert, informing you that the connection is secure and cannot be viewed or accessed by a third party.

● It is now safe to click on the **OK button**.

Security Alert

You are about to view pages over a secure connection.

Any information you exchange with this site cannot be viewed by anyone else on the Web.

☐ In the future, do not show this warning

OK   More Info

8 SUBMITTING YOUR ORDER

● To send the details to the vendor, click a button that contains the word **Submit** – this is the action that transmits the order.

● It is at this point where most people feel concern when they make their first financial transaction over the internet – your personal details and your credit card number appear to be released into cyberspace for anyone with an internet connection to read. This is emphatically not the case as is fully explained in the following chapter.

● For the moment, it is worth noting the locked padlock symbol at bottom right of the screen 🔒. This indicates that the connection over which your web browser is sending your details is secure and can only be read by the intended recipient.

---

4. Click the Submit Order button

You must click the Submit Order button to complete your order.

Once you click "Submit Order," our fulfillment process begins and no changes can be made to your order.

Remember: Our 100% guarantee ensures that every item you purchase at REI meets your high standards—or you can return it for a replacement or refund. REI.com purchases can be returned at any REI store as well as through REI mail order.

Let us know if you are having problems checking out.

🖹 Done   🔒 🌐 Internet

Locked padlock confirms a secure connection •

OTHER PURCHASING INFORMATION

● In many internet transactions, you receive extra information from the vendor, and you may be asked to provide more information.

● Often you are told whether the item is in stock and, if it isn't, when new inventory is expected.

● You may be asked to choose what form of delivery you would like. This can range from overnight express to normal mail. Depending on the kind of order and the distances involved, you may be told how long the delivery is likely to take.

● If you live in a different country from the vendor, there may be import charges or customs duty to pay.

● The vendor may arrange for you to monitor the progress of your order from the vendor to your address.

---

21 **Security Symbols**

BUYING WITH SECURITY

The biggest factor preventing people from using the internet for buying and selling is the fear that their personal details and credit card numbers become freely available. They don't.

CHECKING A SITE'S SECURITY

When sending your personal details and credit card number to a vendor's site, your details are sent in a coded, or encrypted, form. Websites contain a considerable amount of information about their security, which can be checked very easily.

IDENTIFY A SECURE CONNECTION

● The website chosen here to illustrate how to look at a site's level of protection, **www.sportchalet.com**, is typical of many millions of secure websites. The first indication that this is a secure site is that the address, or URL ("Uniform Resource Locator"), begins with the prefix "**https**" when you enter the information-sensitive areas of a site, and not the more usual "**http**." The extra letter "**s**" stands for secure.

● To find further information about the site's security, first right-click on the web page and then select **Properties**.

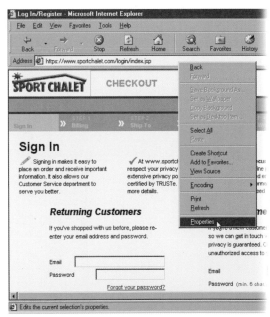

● In the **Properties**
window, the description
of the connection begins
with the letters "**SSL**."
These stand for "Secure
Sockets Layer," a set of rules
for secure communication.

● Although the 40 bit
encryption is described as
"**Low**," this means that a
computer processing 64
million instructions a
second would take a year to
break the encryption.

● The details you send take
only milliseconds to reach
their destination, making
interception difficult.

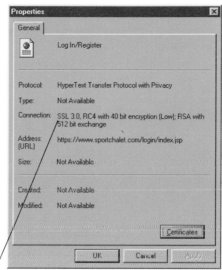

The SSL type of connection ●

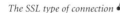

VIEWING CERTIFICATES

● Responsible and
trustworthy websites hold
certificates that are issued
by licensed certification
authorities. A list of the
licensed authorities in the
US can be found on the
State Department's website
at **www.secstate.wa.gov/ea/
ca_lic.htm**.

● To view a website's
certificates, click the
Certificates button in the
Properties window.

● The **General** tab in the **Certificates** window shows that the certificate has been issued to the website URL.

● If the URL in your browser matches the name in the certificate, you are dealing with a safe and secure operator.

How security certificates work

Your computer receives a certificated site's "public" encryption key, which encrypts the details you send to the site. The site decodes your details with its own "private" encryption key, which is the only method of decoding.

SECURE SHOPPING GUARANTEE

● So far, we have seen that **sportchalet.com** receives your details over a connection that is securely encrypted. To discover further details, click on the site's **Secure Shopping Guarantee**.

In addition to all the protection we have seen so far, sportchalet.com also provides a guarantee

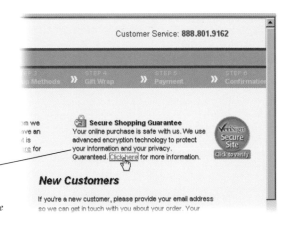

● The Guarantee Details remind you, the prospective purchaser, that the Fair Credit Billing Act in the US limits your liabilities of any fraudulent charges to $50.00.

● Based on the level of security that the company has incorporated into their website, they are in a position to promise that they will cover that $50.00 liability for any unauthorized purchases made through their website.

● The combination of the security level and the guarantee, make this, and many other similar sites, very safe places to shop.

● To close the Guarantee window, click on its Close button at top right.

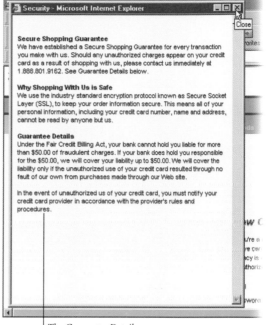

The Guarantee Details

VERISIGN SECURE SITE

● The certification authority in the case of **sportchalet. com** is Verisign, which can be found listed on the State Department's website referred to earlier ☐.

● Finally, click on the logo to confirm the details of the site.

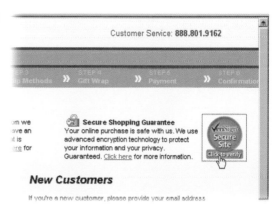

● The **Verisign Secure Site** confirmation page reiterates the fact that the certificate is valid and has indeed been issued to **sportchalet.com**.

● The confirmation page also contains information concerning **sportchalet.com**'s physical location, the name of the company,

whose site it is, and provides further details about the identity of the server that houses the site in question.

VeriSign
The Sign of Trust on the Net®

WWW.SPORTCHALET.COM is a VeriSign Secure Site

Security remains the primary concern of on-line consumers. The VeriSign Secure Site Program allows you to learn more about web sites you visit before you submit any confidential information. Please verify that the information below is consistent with the site you are visiting.

Name	WWW.SPORTCHALET.COM
Status	**Valid**
Validity Period	20-Oct-2000 - 17-Nov-2001
Server ID Information	Country = US State = California Locality = La Canada Organization = Sport Chalet, Inc Organizational Unit = imogene-sch-40 Organizational Unit = Terms of use at www.verisign.com/rpa (c)00 Common Name = www.sportchalet.com

If the information is correct, you may submit sensitive data (e.g., credit card numbers) to this site with the assurance that:

- This site has a VeriSign Secure Server ID.
- VeriSign has verified the organizational name and that SPORT CHALET, INC has the proof of right to use it.
- This site legitimately runs under the auspices of SPORT CHALET, INC.
- All information sent to this site, if in an SSL session, is encrypted, protecting against disclosure to third parties.

To ensure that this is a legitimate VeriSign Secure Site, make sure that:

THAWTE.COM

● Thawte, which was acquired by Verisign in December 1999, is a similar organization to Verisign. Thawte can provide SSL certificates and SuperCerts to provide proof of identity of the owner of a website. The company also provides the facilities for software developers to sign their products as proof of authenticity, and issues free personal certificates to protect emails.

The Thawte organization can be found at www.thawte.com.

NON-ENCRYPTED WEBSITES

Encryption should not be used as the final criterion by which to judge a website. There are many thousands of sites that have no need to be encrypted. This is because they contain neither the facilities to complete order forms, nor the connections to accept payments. Directories, such as this list of Madison Avenue stores, **www.madisonavenuenyc. com**, list websites of stores and businesses, and provide links to them. The fact that sites such as these are not encrypted does not mean that they are suspect in any way.

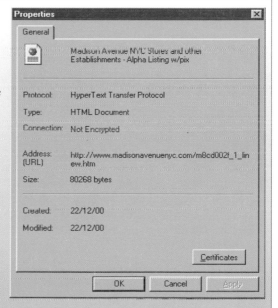

PASSWORDS

Passwords are an almost universally favored method on websites for preventing other people from accessing your personal account details.

An important factor to remember when choosing a password is not to use a plain, simple number directly that can be easily connected to you, such as your date of birth, house number, or your telephone number. House and telephone numbers are also to be avoided because they are likely to change in the future.

CHOOSING PASSWORDS

● Ideally, you should create a new password for each new site that you join, or account that you open online, and not write them down anywhere. Unless you possess a memory that you could make money from, this is often an unachievable ideal.

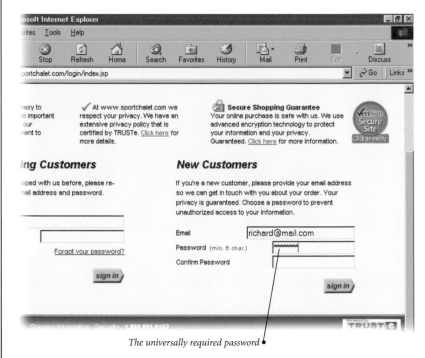

The universally required password ●

● However, one method used is to take one of the numbers connected to you, and use it indirectly by selecting letters from the name of the website on the basis of that number. For example, if you were born on November 27, 1969, your password for **sportchalet.com** could be "ssphslcl" (11271969). For added security, combine your birth date with another anniversary as a further method of creating your own encryption key

1 2 3 4 5 6 7 8 9
S P O R T C H A L E T . C O M

1 1 2 7 1 9 6 9
S S P H S L C L

An encryption key is the device you use to lock (i.e., encrypt) and unlock your password. In this example, the key is your date of birth. To unlock this password, someone would first have to possess two of your passwords from two different identified sites before they could begin to work out the method of encryption you are using.

SECURITY SYMBOLS

A security symbol appears at the foot of your browser window when viewing secure pages. Internet Explorer displays a padlock near the bottom right of the screen, as shown here. If the padlock is closed, the page is secure, and any information that you enter into it is protected. If you are using Netscape Navigator, the secure-page symbol is either a padlock or a key, depending on which version of Netscape you are using.

If the key symbol is displayed broken, or the padlock is open, then the site is not secure. The site is only secure when the padlock is closed.

You should note, though, that usually you are not on the secure area of a website until you begin to enter your credit card information, so it is likely that the secure symbols may not be present when you first enter a site.

Internet Explorer's security symbol is at bottom right.

Netscape Navigator's security symbol is at bottom left.

ALTERNATIVE PAYMENT METHODS

There is a very large number of alternative methods of paying for goods and services on the internet. This is mainly because many companies have attempted to establish a payment method that they hope will be secure, accepted, and profitable. Here, we look at two of the options – SET and Tradenable.

SECURE ELECTRONIC TRANSACTION

● Secure Electronic Transaction (SET) is a method of payment that imitates the existing credit card payment methods and prevents the seller from seeing the credit card details. It uses cryptographic methods, again based on public keys, and digital certificates that guarantee confidentiality of both the payment and the ordering information ⌐.

● Before allowing any transaction to take place, the system authenticates that a cardholder is a legitimate user of an account and that a merchant is a legitimate seller of a product or service. Only sites displaying the SET logo can use this system, which, it is hoped, may become the standard method of payment over the internet.

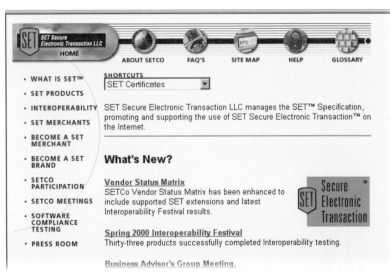

*An immense amount of data about Secure Electronic Transaction can be found at **http://setco.org**.*

TRADENABLE

- This organization offers to act as an intermediary between sellers and buyers in deals involving tangible, physical goods.

- Once you are registered with Tradenable and have an account, either as a buyer or a seller, you can start a new sale at any time. The Tradenable fee is paid for by the buyer or the seller, or split equally between them, depending on their agreement.

- Once this agreement has been reached, Tradenable notifies the buyer to pay Tradenable by either credit card, personal check, business check, money order, cashier's check, or wire transfer.

- When the payment is received, Tradenable notifies the seller to ship the goods to the buyer. The buyer inspects the goods and notifies Tradenable that they are acceptable. Tradenable then pays the seller. In addition, Tradenable has the mechanisms in place to deal with any kind of dispute that might arise.

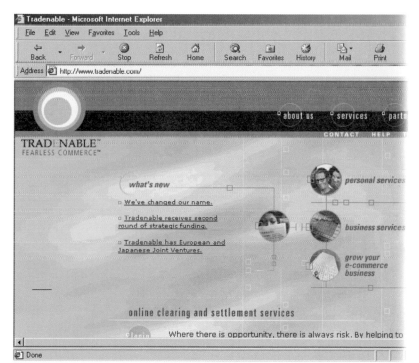

*Tradenable's address is **www.tradenable.com**.*

DEALING IN CONFIDENCE

There is widespread awareness among governmental and other agencies that the general lack of confidence in the security of the internet is seriously holding back the development of ecommerce. Sites are being developed to supply that confidence.

BETTER BUSINESS BUREAU

● The Better Business Bureau has been in existence since the early 20th century, with the aim of encouraging self-regulation and ethical business practises. One of their websites: **www.bbbonline.org**, is designed to help both businesses and consumers with conducting deals across the internet.

● One of the ways in which the organization assists the consumer is to issue the unique BBBOnLine Reliability seal. This is awarded only to those companies that meet the rigorous standards set by the Better Business Bureau.

● When a site displays this seal, consumers can be sure that they are dealing with a legitimate website and, behind it, a highly responsible company.

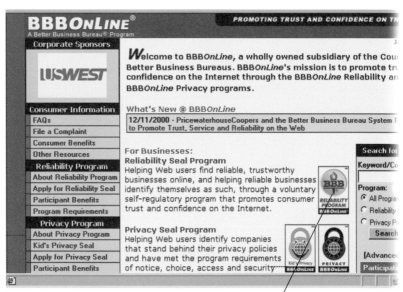

Reliability seal ●

WHOIS.NET

● Among the services provided by this site is the means to discover the location, the individuals involved, and many other details about a website by entering the significant part of its URL into a field.

● Here, to verify and expand what we know about **sportchalet**, enter the name and click on **Go!**

● The contact details of **sportchalet.com** are provided in great detail.

● **Whois.net** is a very useful tool for verifying that you are dealing with a legitimate and trustworthy website, such as **sportchalet.com**.

WHOIS information for sportchalet.com:

Registrar: NETWORK SOLUTIONS, INC.

Organization: Sport Chalet, Inc
address: 920 Foothill Blvd
La Canada, CA 91011 US

Admin contact: Sympson, Laura
email: SPCHWWW@AOL.COM
phone: 818 7902717243
fax:

Tech contact: Miller, R
email: millerr@GLOBALSPORTSINC.COM
phone: 610 4917066
fax: 610 2928766

Nameservers: ns.digisle.net
ns1.digisle.net

Lookup another domain: [   ] Submit

GOOD TRADERS LISTS

● There are many Good Traders lists on the web, such as the **Sportscards Good Trader List** shown here. These sites can be found by entering "**good traders**" in a search engine. Often created by people with a common interest, these lists are the simplest, and often a very reliable, form of recommendation, since they're based on positive experiences.

● Some sites also include Bad Traders lists, which can be equally useful.

HELP WITH BAD TRADERS

One of the first sites to visit if you have the misfortune to encounter a bad trader is **www.traderlist.com**. This site contains a large number of helpful and informative advice pages that provide virtually every conceivable link that you could need to report, and take action over, a bad trader. For example, **/Helplinks. html** provides a large number of links to help you track your order, how to check a dealer's location with zip code lookup, how to report mail fraud to the US Postal Inspection Service, and how to report fraud to government agencies.

BEANIE TRADERS

This site, **www.webebeans.com/traders.html**, has almost 200,000 members, links to countless auctions, and connections to 300 dealers' websites. "Good Traders Resource" is clearly an understatement here.

FACTORS TO REMEMBER

METHOD OF PAYMENT

If you decide to pay by credit card or charge card, your transaction is protected by the Fair Credit Billing Act. If you are not comfortable entering your credit or charge card account number online, call it in to the company's 800 number, or fax it.

PHYSICAL LOCATION

To help avoid overseas or offshore scams, find out where a company is actually located. Are the physical address and contact numbers displayed on the website? If not, ask or find out its address and phone number. You should then be able to check out the company with outside organizations, such as the Better Business Bureau and other consumer agencies.

PRINT YOUR ORDER DETAILS

Keep printed paper records of your transactions. Print out the address of the company site you are dealing with. In addition, it is vital to print out a copy of your order, including the confirmation numbers, and save it at least until the merchandise arrives.

PRIVACY

Companies who are approved to participate in the BBBOnLine Privacy Program must display their privacy policies, conform to the BBB's privacy principles, and allow themselves to be subject to monitoring and review.

REFUNDS AND RETURNS POLICY

The vendor's refund and return policy should always be posted on its website – even if its policy is one of no returns. Make sure you know the policy before you place an order.

SITES TO AVOID

It would be foolish to pretend that every website on the world wide web is a model of probity and rectitude. The web attracts the dishonest, as does any moneymaking opportunity. Here is an example of the type of site to avoid, and the reasons why.

WARNING SIGNALS

❶ Presentation
Scam business sites are often full of capital letters, dollar signs, and exclamation points. It's also not uncommon for these ads to include misspellings and grammatical errors.

❷ The site's URL
*If the site's URL doesn't look legitimate, don't buy from it. Look for the prefix **https://** in the address bar to be sure that the site is secure, and beware of trading sites without it ⬚. Be suspicious of any commercial website's URL that contains a ~ (tilde). This symbol sometimes indicates personal web space within a larger, unidentified site.*

❸ Delivery time
The laws that apply to phone or mail shopping also apply to internet transactions. A company must ship an order within 30 days, or the time stated in its ads if that period is shorter.

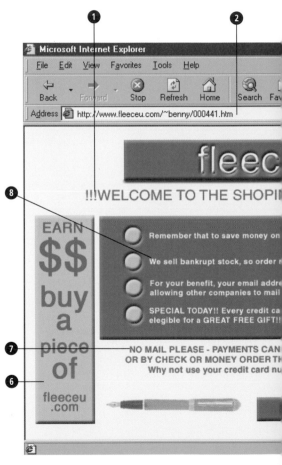

14 **Identify a Secure Connection**

ONLINE SCAM STORIES

One site that documents online scams in detail is: **www.traderlist.com/ scambusters.html**. Although the site concentrates on fraud involving beanies and Barbie dolls, the stories are highly illustrative of what can happen.

WARNING SIGNALS

4 Privacy policy
Check a company's privacy policy to make sure that it doesn't sell its customers' details to other companies.

5 Account details
Never give out your checking account, credit card number, or personal information unless you're certain that a company is legitimate.

6 Appeals to greed
"Get Rich Quick" schemes have no place on responsible websites. The immediacy of the internet has made it easy for the criminally minded to reach eager buyers and convince them that dollars invested in an internet business will rapidly multiply.

7 Payment methods
If a seller asks for payment in cash by private courier, or by check or money order through an overnight delivery service, be extremely suspicious. The company is attempting to circumvent the laws designed to prevent postal fraud.

8 Pressurized selling
Beware of pressure for an immediate response or claims of limited availability. Any responsible company gives you time to make your own decisions.

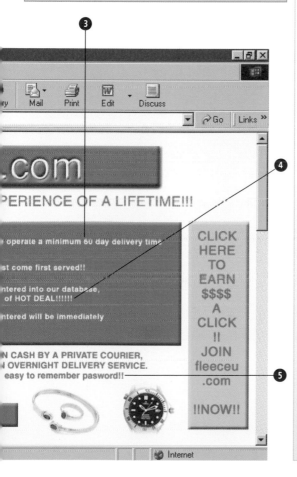

USING ONLINE AUCTIONS

Auctions on the internet have flourished since they first appeared in 1995. Different kinds of auctions have evolved to meet different needs, and they provide a virtual global market.

WHY USE AUCTIONS?

Internet auctions contain an almost infinite variety of merchandise available from around the world. They act as a storefront for sellers, who can be either individuals or large organizations, to market their wares worldwide.

THE NEW YARD SALE
● There is a wide range of collectibles and antiques for sale at auction sites. Online auction sites allow sellers to post many kinds of small items for sale, from software packages to comic books to jewelry. If you're looking for the kind of merchandise that used to be found only at a yard sale or flea market, the internet is a vast and invaluable collecting resource.

www.4auctiondeals.com is one of the many auction sites on the internet.

Types of Auctions

Internet auctions are bazaars. In most cases, sellers offer one item at a time, but sometimes sellers offer multiple lots of the same item. The auction websites often refer to auctions of multiple items as "Dutch" or "English" auctions. At some sites, the seller may be required to sell all items at the price of the lowest successful bid. At other sites, the seller is entitled to the prices bid by each highest bidder.

BUSINESS AUCTION SITES

● Business auctions can be business-to-business or business-to-consumer auction sites. Operators of these sites have physical control of the merchandise because in most cases they own what is on offer. They are in a position to accept payment in many different forms for the goods.

www.dealdeal.com is a business auction site offering equipment they themselves have control over.

PERSON-TO-PERSON AUCTION SITES

● In person-to-person auctions, individual sellers or small businesses offer their items for auction directly to consumers. The organizations operating the auction site do not own the goods, but provide the auction service.

Playle's Online Auctions (www.playle.com) is a straightforward person-to-person auction site.

REVERSE AUCTION SITES

● With reverse auction sites, you enter the details of what you want and how much you are prepared to pay for it. The reverse auctioneer then forwards your request to its pool of suppliers. A supplier may respond by matching your request, say that they can't match it, or that they are able to match it but at a higher price, which may start a bidding process.

● One obvious problem with reverse auction sites is that many of your requests may not find any matches.

● Another problem over which you have little control is that your request and personal details are sent to numerous companies. Therefore, it is a good idea to check the privacy policies of the individual auction sites.

● Choose those sites that place responses to your requests into an account you can check, rather than advertise your email address to anyone who might be interested.

www.ewanted.com *is one of the reputable reverse auction sites.*

RESERVE PRICE AUCTIONS

● It is very common that when a seller offers a piece of merchandise for sale in an internet auction, the site allows them to set a reserve price below which they will not sell. The site announces that a reserve price exists, but without publishing it.

● To win the auction, a bidder must meet or exceed the reserve price, and be the highest bidder. If no one meets the reserve price, neither the seller nor the highest bidder have any further obligations.

www.hamquest.com is one of the auction websites that allows sellers to set a reserve price.

DUTCH AUCTIONS

● These auctions are popular with people who have many identical items to sell. Sellers post a minimum starting bid, and the quantity for sale. Bidders specify a price and the quantity they want.

● All winning bidders pay the same price – the lowest successful bid, which might be less than some of them bid. If the requested items exceed those available, the earliest successful bidders get the quantities they asked for. Later bidders may be offered a smaller quantity than they bid for, but are allowed to refuse.

www.vrbid.com conduct several auction formats – including Dutch auctions, which are the most difficult to understand.

How to Find Merchandise

With the many hundreds of auction sites available on the internet, checking every one for an item that you're looking for is not a feasible proposition. The alternative is to use a search engine dedicated exclusively to auction sites.

LOGGING ON TO BIDDER'S EDGE

- By far the most comprehensive auction search engine is BidXS. To find it, type: **www.bidxs.com** in the address bar of your browser window.
- In addition to having a directory-based structure, there is also the possibility of searching by keyword. Type in your selected keyword, in the example shown here, **boxing glove**, and click on GO!

FINDING AN ITEM

- The search results contain a total of 44 items, including a glove signed by the British heavyweight boxer, Lennox Lewis. The details show that the auction is being conducted by Yahoo!, the price is $25.00, and the time the auction closes is given. Double-clicking on the entry in which you're interested reveals the details.

VIEWING THE DETAILS
- The details screen contains a wealth of information about the auction of this item.
- Among the important factors are the types of payment accepted and the shipping arrangements; i.e., the buyer pays the shipping costs, and the item is then shipped on full payment.

- It is possible to join the auction by signing up with Yahoo!, but because we are testing the waters, we'll leave this until we know how to buy at auction.

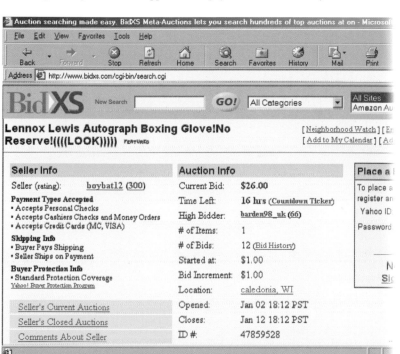

OTHER AUCTION SEARCH ENGINES

http://search.auctionwatch.com/usearch/ AuctionWatch features news and information, and a very active message center where people exchange views and stories of online auction experiences.

http://www.globalonline.com/ globalauction.asp Global Online has access to more than 80 online auctions. It includes global news and stocks, and a price-comparison engine.

How to Buy at Auction

To bid on items at most sites, you first need to register, and choose a user name and password. The steps that follow include finding the merchandise, checking the seller's credentials, checking the goods, placing the bid, and following the auction.

REGISTERING WITH EBAY

● eBay is the largest auction site on the internet, and before you can begin trading, you first have to register with them.

● Having located their home page at **www.ebay.com**, click on the **register** button at top right of the eBay home page.

● There are three steps in the registration process: completing the Initial Registration Form; receiving a confirmation code from eBay by email; and finally, sending in a confirmation of your registration.

● You will be making life simpler for yourself, the people you deal with, and eBay if you register in your country of residence.

eBay UK Registration

If you don't currently reside in the United Kingdom, click here.

How to Register - To register on eBay, follow the registration proce complete all three steps, you can begin buying and selling on eBay.

1) Complete the eBay UK Initial Registration Form - Simply fill below, review your information for accuracy, and click the Submit but

2) Receive Confirmation Instructions - eBay will send you an e-m confirmation code.
If you already have completed step 1 and you need eBay to resend your confi

3) Confirm Your Registration - Once you have your access code (finalize your registration by accepting the eBay UK User Agreement

● The registration process, which is very short, concludes with eBay displaying its own confirmation that you have been registered.

Welcome to eBay UK! You are now registered!

Thank you for completing your eBay UK registration. Your registration is confirmed. Please discard your temporary access code - it is no longer necessary and you can password now.

SEARCHING FOR MERCHANDISE

● Back at eBay's home page, there is a search facility similar to the Bidder's Edge site.

● Here, the search can be resumed for the boxing glove, and when the search terms have been entered, click on **Find it!**

SELECTING AN ITEM

● Lennox Lewis's glove has reappeared among the 108 similar items that eBay has up for auction, but the price is now $60.00. As no bids have been made, the price of $60.00 is a public reserve price set by the seller. The abbreviation "w/COA" means "with certificate of authenticity."

● Click on the entry to find the page that contains further details.

108 items found for "**boxing glove**". Showing items 1 to 50.   Sort: Items ending first

All items	All items including Gallery preview	Gallery items only			
Item#	**Featured Items**		Price	Bids	Ends

There are no featured items within these search results.
To find out how to be listed in this section and seen by thousands, please visit this link Featured Auctions

Item#	**Current Items**	Price	Bids	Ends
540142531	Boxing Glove Genuine Block Meerschaum Pipe	$7.50	1	Jan-1
1107706411	DOUBLE BOXING GLOVE CASE SOLID OAK AND ACRYL	$39.95	-	Jan-1
1107716063	Maury Povich auto Boxing Glove w/coa	$24.99	-	Jan-1
1107357912	LENNOX LEWIS signed Boxing Glove (w/COA) Buy It Now	$60.00	-	Jan-1

CHECKING THE SELLER

● The page detailing the goods contains a quantity of other useful information, including the seller's user ID. In this case it is "autographs99," which almost certainly indicates a dealer, who most likely bought the glove at the Yahoo! auction and is now offering it for resale – at a profit, naturally.

● On this page appears what is called the **seller's Feedback Profile**. This can be clicked on to view the experiences of others who have dealt with this particular seller.

● It is worth checking these experiences if any are available, irrespective of whether the seller appears to be a trading dealer or a private individual.

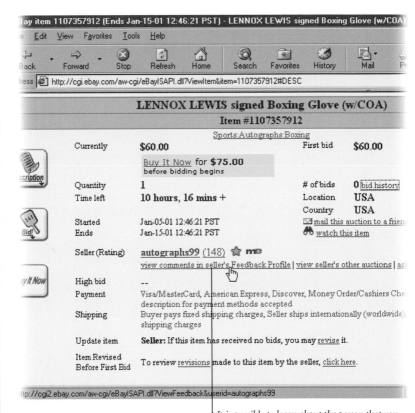

It is possible to learn about the person that you want to do business with by checking this profile

● In this case, the seller has more than 150 positive responses. This total number of responses can be taken as confirmation that autographs99 is both a dealer and one that can be trusted.

● Scrolling down the page reveals a list of written comments from previous satisfied buyers.
● It is worth paying attention to this feedback because each of these buyers has had to make a conscious effort to sign in, go to the Feedback area, and enter their comments. No one would bother to go to these lengths unless they were genuinely impressed.

Comments from previous buyers

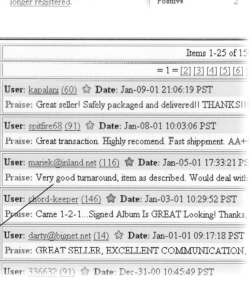

CHECKING THE GOODS

● If the seller is highly recommended, as is the case here, this is a definite encouragement to proceed.

● The next element to check is a photograph of the glove, contained in the main page for this item. Photographs of items offered at auction are now so common that many people will not buy merchandise if there is no illustration to accompany the sale.

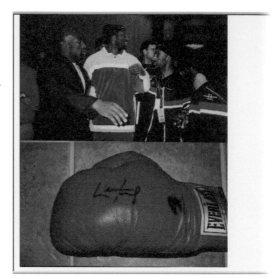

PLACING THE BID

● Scroll down to the foot of the screen and view the bidding area. The minimum price set by the seller of $60.00 is the opening bid. Enter your maximum bid, in this case $65.00, and eBay bids up to that figure on your behalf without allowing any other bidder to know your maximum bid; this is known as proxy bidding.

● Note also that the opportunity exists with this item to end the auction by buying the glove for $75.00.

● After entering your bid, click on **Review bid**.

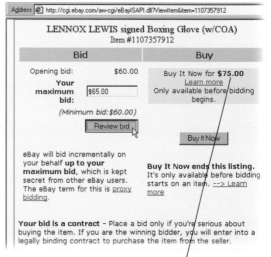

Buying at this price ends the auction ●

● The **Review and Confirm** screen shows that the current bid is $60.00. If there are no other bidders, then that is what the glove will be bought for. eBay asks you to enter your User ID and password, which were set up during the registration procedure, and finally to confirm your bid by clicking on **Place bid**.

● It is very important not to bid on an item that you do not intend to buy. If you are the highest bidder when the auction closes, you have an obligation to buy the goods. Auction companies eventually bar nonpaying bidders from future bidding, and you may experience difficulties elsewhere, particularly if you email the seller, reveal your identity, and then renege on the deal.

Address 🔗 http://cgi.ebay.com/aw-cgi/eBayISAPI.dll

Review and confirm your bid:
Item #1107357912 LENNOX LEWIS signed Boxing Glove (w/COA)

Confirm that your bid is correct, enter your eBay User ID and password, and click the 'Place bid' button.

Your current bid: **$60.00**

Your maximum bid: $65.00

Your User ID:	latitude51uk
	You can also use your email address.
Your Password:	********
	Forgot your password?

Are you tired of typing in your User ID and Password over and over again? Save time by signing in. (You may also sign in securely).

[Place bid]

Click here if you wish to cancel

eBay will bid incrementally on your behalf up to your maximum bid, which is kept secret from other eBay users. The eBay to bidding.

🔗

PRINT OUT EVERYTHING

During the course of an auction, you will see a lot of information. It is more than useful to save all the information that you see onscreen, and which is generated by your transaction.

Print out the seller's ID, the description of the goods, and note the date and price you bid on the item. In addition, print every email you may send or receive from the seller.

USING MY EBAY

Placing a bid in an auction is far from being the end of the affair, because the auction continues until the predetermined closing time. You'll be interested in following the progress of the bidding, and My eBay makes it easy to keep in touch.

● eBay congratulates you on being the current high bidder, and suggests that you keep track of your bids by looking at My eBay, which can only be seen by you, the bidder.

● Click on the **My eBay** link to access this option.

Yes - although you are currently the high bidder, this does not guarantee you will win this auction. Another you, so check back before the auction ends or allow eBay to bid on your behalf (how this works). If you are notify you by email. **Don't want to be contacted** — You may also customize your notification preference

Keeping track of your bids
You can keep track of your bids by looking at your My eBay page. My eBay provides a convenient at-a- activity page accessible only by you. Try it now! It's free.

● Enter your user ID and password in the first page, and click on **enter**.

Your User ID: latitude51uk

You can also use your email address.

Your Password: ••••••••

Forgot your password?

Are you tired of typing in your User ID and Password over and over again? Save time by signing in. (You may also sign in securely).

Press [enter] to enter My eBay.

● Your own private My eBay screen appears, containing all the details of your current, active bids. The bid price is shown in green, indicating that the $60.00 is the leading bid.

Show current items and items ending within the last [2] days (30 days

Items I'm Bidding On					
Item	Start Price	Current Price	My Max Bid	Quantity	#
LENNOX LEWIS signed Boxing Glove (w/COA)					
1107357912	$60.00	$60.00	$65.00	N/A	
Item	Start Price	Current Price	My Max Bid	Quantity	#
Totals: 1	$60.00	$60.00		N/A	

• You can return to the My eBay screen at any time by clicking on the **My eBay** link at the top of eBay's main page.

RETURNING TO THE BIDDING

● If you return to the bidding, you can see the effect that your bid has had. Here, a minimum bid increment of $1.00 has appeared, and the minimum bid is now $61.00.

● The **Buy It Now** option has now been withdrawn because bidding on the glove has started.

The new minimum bid increment

Biddin

LENNOX LEWIS signed Boxing Glove (w/CO
Item #110735/912

Current bid:	$60.00
Bid increment:	$1.00
Your maximum bid:	

(Minimum bid: $61.00)

Review bid

eBay will bid incrementally on your behalf **up to your maxi**
which is kept secret from other eBay users. The eBay term
proxy bidding.

Your bid is a contract – Place a bid only if you're serious
buying the item. If you are the winning bidder, you will ent
legally binding contract to purchase the item from the selle

Buy It Now no longer available – This item was listed wit
Now price which is no longer available since bidding has sta
Learn more

ENDING THE AUCTION

When the closing time of the auction has passed, return to My eBay to learn the result. The My eBay screen indicates that the auction has ended and the winning bid is again shown in green.

The procedures that follow the conclusion of an auction vary from auction site to auction site, but it is usually the case that you and the seller receive each other's name and email address, and it's up to you to complete the transaction from there on.

SELLING ONLINE

There are many methods that you can use to sell online. This section looks at placing classified ads on the web, selling at auction, and creating and promoting your own website.

USING WEB CLASSIFIEDS

The internet now contains a very large number of sites carrying free classified advertising. Here we look at an antiques site, a motorized vehicle site, and two more general sites, each of which requires a different method of posting your classified ad. All these sites require you to register, but most make doing so very easy.

USING A CLASSIFIED ANTIQUES SITE

● Of the many sales sites, **www.antiqueclassifiedad.com** is a good place to start if you have an antique of any kind to sell.

● When you arrive at the site, start the process of placing an ad by clicking on the **Post** tab at the top of the main page.

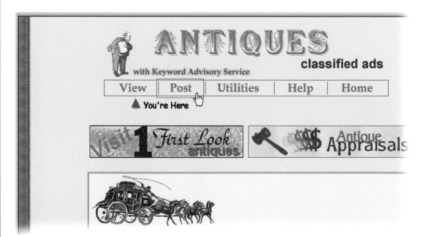

● The first part of the **Posting New AD** page consists of checking the category of antique that you want to sell and specifying how long you want your ad to be displayed. The next part involves completing the registration information including your personal details and a password 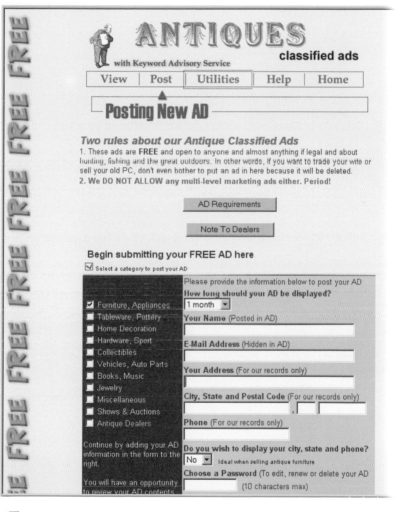.

ANTIQUES
with Keyword Advisory Service   **classified ads**

| View | Post | Utilities | Help | Home |

Posting New AD

Two rules about our Antique Classified Ads

1. These ads are **FREE** and open to anyone and almost anything if legal and about hunting, fishing and the great outdoors. In other words, if you want to trade your wife or sell your old PC, don't even bother to put an ad in here because it will be deleted.
2. We DO NOT ALLOW any multi-level marketing ads either. Period!

AD Requirements

Note To Dealers

Begin submitting your FREE AD here

☑ Select a category to post your AD

☑ Furniture, Appliances
☐ Tableware, Pottery
☐ Home Decoration
☐ Hardware, Sport
☐ Collectibles
☐ Vehicles, Auto Parts
☐ Books, Music
☐ Jewelry
☐ Miscellaneous
☐ Shows & Auctions
☐ Antique Dealers

Continue by adding your AD information in the form to the right.

You will have an opportunity to review your AD contents.

Please provide the information below to post your AD
How long should your AD be displayed?
[1 month ▾]

Your Name (Posted in AD)
[   ]

E-Mail Address (Hidden in AD)
[   ]

Your Address (For our records only)
[   ]

City, State and Postal Code (For our records only)
[   ] , [   ] [   ]

Phone (For our records only)
[   ]

Do you wish to display your city, state and phone?
[No ▾] Ideal when selling antique furniture

Choose a Password (To edit, renew or delete your AD
[   ] (10 characters max)

20 Choosing Passwords

● Further down the page is the opportunity to specify the headline for your advertisement and a panel for the text of your advertisement. This allows you to describe in detail the item, its price, and any shipping arrangements that are required.

● Once you have completed and checked these details, click the **Submit** button once, and your ad is posted. The site informs you when a buyer has been found and then puts you in contact with one another.

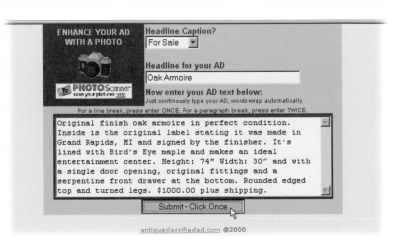

USING A DIRECTORY-BASED SITE

● Another kind of classified ad site is based on a directory structure. **www. traderonline.com** deals in vehicles of all kinds. While an antiques site needs the seller to specify the item at length, due to the variety available, the makes and models of automotive vehicles are much more limited, and a directory makes more sense. Begin by clicking **Place An Ad**.

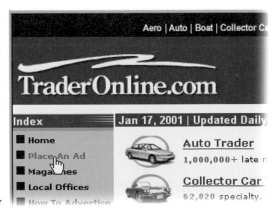

● The essence of a directory-based site is that you simply have to click to move to the next page rather than having to enter an exhaustive description of the merchandise.

● If you are selling a standard automobile, click on **Auto**.

● The following page highlights the fact that there are "**6 easy steps**" for you to follow to submit your ad. The site makes it easy for you to know how far you've progressed through the operation by highlighting the current location in red.

● At this location, select the make, click **Continue**, and follow the same procedure on the subsequent pages until you reach the end of the process.

HALF.COM AND AMAZON.COM

Whatever you want to sell, there is almost certainly an appropriate website that you can find. Antiques and powered transport vehicles are simply examples. However, the different ways in which the sites work can be unexpected, as these two sites show.

HALF.COM

● This site is a fixed-price, online marketplace where you can trade "previously owned" merchandise. The site tends to concentrate on books, music, movies, and games. The reason why these are the preferred items becomes clearer when you see how the site works.

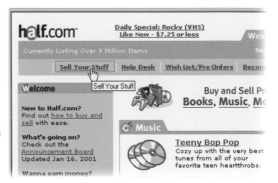

● First there's the appropriate link to click, in this case **Sell Your Stuff**.

● Instead of typing a description of the item as at the antiques site, or clicking through a set of pages to specify the automobile as with the vehicle site, at **half.com** you enter a book's ISBN (International Standard Book Number), or a UPC (Universal Product Code). ISBNs are to be found on a book's dust jacket or on the page following the title page. The UPC of a movie on DVD, for example, is the sequence of numbers around the bar code on the case.

● Type in the number, in this case an ISBN, and click on **Continue**.

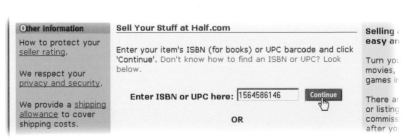

THE BOOK'S DETAILS

● The following screen immediately displays the title of the book, its author, when it was published, and its list price, which have all been found from the ISBN. And all these details appear above an image of the book's dust jacket.

● However, you have to insert the condition of the book yourself. **half.com** has preset descriptions: **Like New**; **Very Good**; **Good**; **Acceptable**; and **Tattered and Torn.** If an item is given this last description, they will refuse to sell it.

● The **Notes** field is for more remarks concerning the item. When the details about the condition have been completed, click on the **Continue** button.

● The inevitable process of registering is now carried out. Following that, your item is posted on the site.

● The shipping arrangements at **half.com** are that the seller must agree to cover the up-front costs, for which **half.com** will reimburse the seller, and then charge the buyer for these costs.

AMAZON.COM

● As the world's largest online bookstore, **amazon.com** is naturally best known for selling books. However, not many people know that it is also possible to use **amazon.com** to sell your own books, providing that **amazon.com** itself sells the book.

● After logging on to **www.amazon.com**, click on the **Books** tab at the top of the window, enter the title of the book that you want to sell in the **Search** field, and click on **GO!**

Click on the Books tab to access this area ●

● Due to the very large number of books that **amazon.com** sells, the number of results is likely to be large.

● When you have scrolled though the list of hits and located your book, click on the book title.

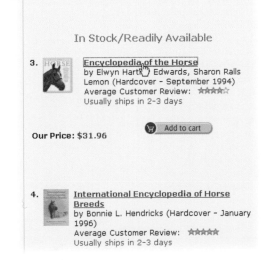

● The information screen for the book appears. Once you have checked that the correct book is displayed, click on the button at the foot of the screen that invites you to **Sell yours here**.

Begin the sale of your book by clicking here

● The following screen asks you to verify that this is the book to be sold; tells you what information you need to provide about price and payment; and asks you to supply a description of the condition of the book in much the same way as **half.com** does ⌐.

● When you have completed these requests, click on **Continue**.

List your item in 60 seconds. Details
Listing is free--here's what we need:

1. **The condition of your item**
   You can add a few words to describe your item.

2. **Your selling price**
   You'll also receive a credit to help cover shipping

3. **Credit card, billing address, and phone** (we only need t
   Your buyer will pay online. This lets us authorize you to receive f

4. **Finally, have a check handy** (we only need this the first
   Your check number will tell us where to deposit your earnings. W
   credit, and transfer your money to you.

What's the condition of your item?
Please choose from the dropdown menu below. You may select "colle
rare. Review our condition guidelines.

Condition: | Used - Very Good ▼ |

Continue ▶

The Book's
Details
49

● The similarities with **half.com** continue with the chance to enter comments describing the condition of the book in more detail.

● After reading the commission, shipping details, and the pricing advice, you can enter the price that you want for

the book. Finally, enter a valid ZIP code; indicate whether you will ship internationally; and click on **Continue**.

Add your comments
Please add a short comment to better describe the condition of your item.

> Minimal marks on dust jacket

70 character limit. Example: Dust cover missing. Some scratches on th front.

Enter the price for your used item
When your item sells, Amazon.com takes a commission of $.99 plus 15% of your sales price, deposits the rest in your account, and gives you the address of your buyer. To help with shipping, Amazon gives you an additional shipping cred More about pricing and fees.

Amazon.com price:	$31.96
Maximum allowable price:	$25.57 (Used items must be priced 20% below the Amazon.com price)
Recommended price:	$19.18 (Based on the condition you indicated)
Current lowest price:	$19.89 (Like New)
Enter your price:	$ $19.00 U.S. Dollars

Location
Please enter a valid U.S. ZIP or Postal Code from which your item will be shipped.

> 98003

Example: 02128

Shipping reimbursement
You must ship your item by standard or surface mail within two business days of purchase. Your shipping credit for addresses within the United States will be $2.20. If you indicate you will ship internationally and your buyer is outside th United States, you will receive a $12.00 international shipping credit. Details

☑ I will ship internationally

 Continue ▶

● The following and subsequent screens concern the **Sign In** process, which has to be done. When finished, your book is online, and is up for sale with **amazon.com**.

Sign In
We ask you to sign in to protect your credit card and other personal info

Enter your e-mail address:

○ I do not have an Amazon.com p

SELLING AT AUCTION

Auctions are an exciting way to sell your merchandise. You can choose what to sell, submit it to the site, and monitor the progress of the bids as frequently as you wish. The process is not unlike a computer game – except that you can earn money.

LAUNCHING THE AUCTION

● The auction site chosen here to illustrate selling at auction is **www.qxl.com**, a European operation, but one that has a little way to go before it rivals eBay.

● All auction sites broadly follow the same series of steps to post merchandise. After going through the usual registration process, you begin by clicking on the **sell** tab on the page.

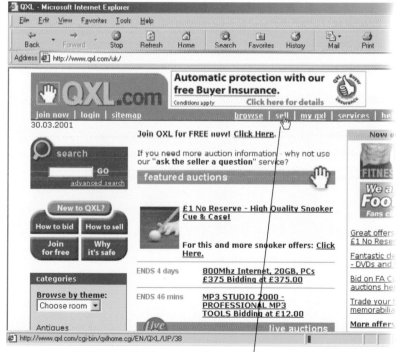

*Clicking the **sell** tab begins the selling process* ●

PRODUCT DESCRIPTION

● After identifying yourself to the site with your member ID and password, you can begin to describe the item you're selling. **Qxl.com**'s method of describing the item for sale requires a main auction title, an optional subtitle, a primary category, and a detailed description.

● Try to anticipate any questions that buyers might have about your merchandise and answer them beforehand in the description of your item.

---

create an auction

Auction Advise

| product description | auction details | location | shipping and payments |

*All fields marked * are mandatory*

*Member ID `latitude51uk`

*Password

*Main Auction Title: `The Encyclopedia of the Horse`

Please enter a concise description here, no more than 40 characters long including spaces). Please do not use HTML tags or (') or (") in your auction title.
eg. John Lennon Signed Photo

Optional Sub-Title:

If you would like further information to appear directly underneath your auction title, enter up to 100 characters (including spaces) here. Please do not use HTML tags or (') or (") in this field.
eg. Rare Photo signed in 1970, authentication included

Would you like your title to appear in bold?

Yes ○ No ●

There is a £1 fee to bold the title of your auction. View full fee <u>details</u>.

*Primary Category:

`Music, Movies & Books - Books - Dictionaries & Encyclopaedias`

Optional Category: (Please choose the categories that best suit your auction. If you place an auction in an inappropriate category, QXL.com reserves the right to remove it.)

`Select Category 2`

*Description: (Write clear, concise, honest descriptions. Use up to 2000 characters - including spaces. Some HTML tags can be included, click on the link below for a list of acceptable HTML.)
<u>What HTML tags can I use?</u>

```
The Encyclopedia of the Horse by
Elwyn H. Edwards. Hardcover.
Published by Dorling Kindersley in
1994. ISBN 1564586146
```

New to QXL?
Your Account
Bidders Guide
Sellers Guide
Before & After Sales
Contact Us

Selling on QXL Follow these four simple steps. Top Sellers, see our <u>Tips</u> page.

① <u>Register</u> with QXL.com in order to be a seller. It's quick and it's free!!!

② <u>Create your auction</u> We'll walk you through the process.

③ <u>Watch the bidding</u> View a sample bid page

④ <u>Collect your winnings</u> We tell you how.

So get started!

Auction Jargon

Start Price
The price at which bidding begins. It's always better to set start price low. The best sellers start auctions at £1.

Reserve Price
The minimum amount you are willing to accept from a bidder. The lower your reserve, the higher your chances of selling.

Bid Increments
The minimum amount your bid will increase by. Setting bid increment of £2, means bids will raise by £2 during each round of bidding.

Minimum Quantity

- Once all the elements of the description have been entered, click on **Next**.

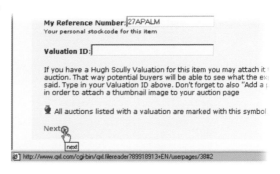

AUCTION DETAILS

- After setting the start date and duration of the auction, the start price and the reserve price can then be established 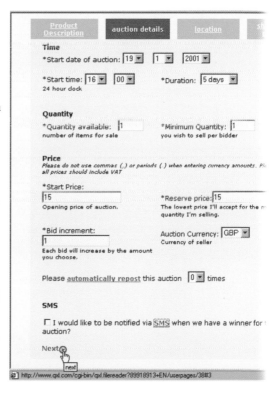. Here, the start and reserve prices are identical, but you can set a low start price to generate some interest, and a higher reserve price to ensure that you receive a minimum fair price.

- The duration of the auction has been set at five days. After that time, you can elect to have your auction reposted (begun again) up to nine times.

- The reference to "SMS" means "Short Message Service," which can be used to notify you of a winning bid on a cellular phone.

- When you're happy with the details you've entered, click on **Next**.

33 **Reserve Price Auctions**

LOCATION

● This tab requires that you first state the country in which the item is located. The condition of the item is required as usual, but the description options are very limited compared to other sites that we've seen.

● Unusually, you have the option of limiting the allowed bidders only to those who hold a credit card. However, there are very few people who browse and become members of the world's auction sites who do not possess a credit card.

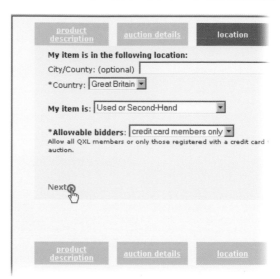

METHODS OF PAYMENT

Usually, you establish the payment options when setting up the auction, so the buyer is aware, from the start, what is available. These options include credit card, debit card, personal check, cashier's check, money order, cash on delivery, and escrow services.

Credit cards offer buyers the greatest consumer protection, including the right to seek a credit from the credit card issuer if the product is not delivered,

or if it bears no resemblance to what was described. Like many sellers in person-to-person auctions, you probably aren't in a position to accept payment by credit card, and you probably require payment by cashier's check or money order before sending the item to the winning bidder.

It is possible for you to use an escrow service where, for a fee of usually five percent of the cost of the item (usually paid by

the buyer), an escrow service accepts payment from the buyer by check, money order, or credit card.

The escrow service informs you when it has received the money, which is released to you, the seller, after the buyer receives and approves the goods. This helps protect buyers from ending up empty-handed after paying their money. However, be aware that using an escrow service can delay the deal.

WHERE TO SHIP, AND WHO PAYS

● The limitations that you can impose on where you are willing to ship items sold at auction are your own decision.

● There are three possible reasons for limiting the shipping area to your own country: first, shipping outside your own country may be more complicated than shipping internally, and will have to involve customs; second, the cost and packing for larger items is not feasible; and third, you may prefer that certain items with a strong national connection and a degree of rarity stay in their country of origin.

● The shipping costs are almost always paid for by the buyer because it is not possible to build shipping costs into the sale price in an auction.

● The buyer may feel more secure if more valuable items are insured during transit. Again, the buyer usually pays these costs, which may only amount to $1 to $2 per $100.00.

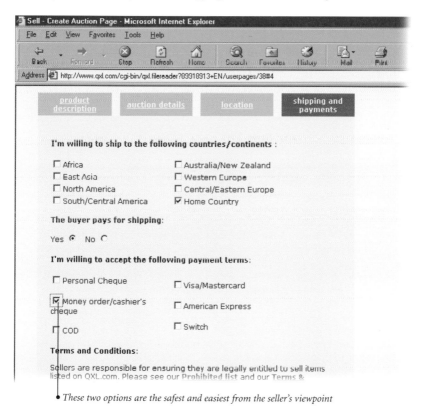

These two options are the safest and easiest from the seller's viewpoint

PAYMENT AND PERCENTAGES

● The payment of a listing fee at the end of an auction is a common practice among online auction houses. The amount varies slightly, but is approximately two percent for the first $15, and a further 2.5 percent for higher amounts.

● At some auction sites, a percentage commission is taken on the sale price, while other sites rely on advertising to maintain their profits.

● The final step is simply to click on **Submit** to start the auction.

☐ Personal Cheque

☑ Money order/cashier's cheque

☐ COD

☐ Visa/Mastercard

☐ American Express

☐ Switch

Terms and Conditions:

Sellers are responsible for ensuring they are legally entitled to sell items listed on QXL.com. Please see our Prohibited list and our Terms & Conditions if you have any questions

Please note: Upon the close of auction, a Listing Fee will be charged.

Submit⊙   Clear⊙

javascript:window.document.forms['CreateProduct'].submit();

END OF THE AUCTION

The bidding for each auction closes at a scheduled time, when the highest bidder wins the auction. As the seller, you will receive the buyer's user ID and email address. With some auction sites, your email address may be sent to the buyer, or may be made available only to the buyer on the website of the auction house.

You need to complete the transaction from that point. Remember that sellers can post feedback about buyers, so don't renege on an auction where you have a successful bidder. Contact the winning bidder as quickly as possible after the auction closes. Confirm the final cost, including any shipping charges, and tell the buyer where to send the payment.

Ship the merchandise as soon as you receive payment. Sellers are required to ship the merchandise within the time frame designated during the auction or, if no time frame is specified, within 30 days.

If you can't meet the shipping commitment for any reason whatsoever, you must give the buyer an opportunity to cancel the order for a full refund, or you must agree a new shipping date.

TIPS FOR SELLERS

COMMUNICATION

Communication is vital for completing successful transactions. Once a deal has been made, provide information on your identity, physical address, and telephone number if you feel comfortable with that.

Keep in touch with the person you are dealing with and don't ignore their emails. Let the buyer know when payment has been received, when the item has been shipped, and of any problems that may have arisen.

Ask your buyer to email you when they have mailed the money. In this way, you will know that the buyer has started their end of the process and you will know when to expect the money.

If you do not hear from the buyer within two days of sending them your address, email them again. Following this, if you have heard nothing from the buyer after a week, email them again, and this time notify them politely that the deal has been canceled.

MERCHANDISE

When advertising your merchandise, be specific and accurate about what it is that you are offering and indicate exactly what condition it is in.

Be honest about your merchandise because all you have is your reputation. Once this has been lost, it is difficult to regain prospective buyers' confidence.

PRICE

Know the worth of your product before you offer it for sale. Look through the various sites for similar items and check the prices. This avoids resentment on your part if you later realize you sold it for too low a price, and prevents it from being overpriced and failing to sell.

PAYMENT

Most sellers ask for payment in advance, either by money order or by check, which is a form of payment that is open to abuse. If you decide to accept a check, tell the buyer that you will need to wait for the check to clear before you can send the merchandise.

SHIPPING

Shipping costs must be mentioned when the item is posted as being for sale, to avoid any confusion over the full and final cost.

Inform your buyer of how you intend to ship the item, and the date when the item should reach its destination.

KEEPING RECORDS

It is wise to keep a hard copy of all the transactions that you take part in. Each time a buyer makes you an offer, note the date, the individual's name, user ID, email address, the merchandise in question, and the price with the full costs. Add the buyer's address to your records when the deal is made and when emails are exchanged.

Record the dates when the buyer mailed the money; when the money was received; when you mailed the goods; and when the package was actually received.

Save all emails relating to a transaction for as long as you feel that they may be needed.

USING YOUR OWN WEBSITE

So far, the methods of selling have used websites created by other people. An alternative is to create your own website to sell your wares and have complete control over what appears on the site, and how it works. Your page can remain on the web for as long as you wish, it can be indexed by search engines, and you can customize and present the information exactly as you want. There are other titles in this "Essential Computers" series to show you how easy it is. Here, we concentrate on what to include in a website that exclusively promotes your merchandise.

THE HOME PAGE

● This sample website is designed to promote a self-published, illustrated children's book, where the writing, design, production, and advertising are controlled entirely by the author. The home page provides a flavor of the book, and immediately gives the price, including the shipping costs.

● Keep the site simple. Make it easy for people to get to your content. Be careful about using animations because, although they can be attractive and eye-catching, they can lose their impact when overused, and slow down the loading time of a page. You're also less likely to lose customers if you keep your pages short by using smaller images.

THE ORDER PAGE

● The kinds of information that can be given here include what form of payment you accept, and the conditions and timescale for delivery of the order. The separate shipping charges can be provided. Give an order number, either on this page or, as here, on a following, confirmatory page.

● Include a link to your privacy policy, which need state little more than the fact that you will not share your customers' details with any third party under any circumstances.

● Most importantly, don't forget to include the fields in which your customers can enter their details.

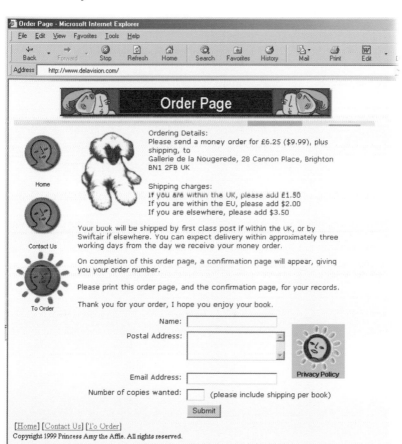

Order Page - Microsoft Internet Explorer

File   Edit   View   Favorites   Tools   Help

Back   Forward   Stop   Refresh   Home   Search   Favorites   History   Mail   Print   Edit

Address   http://www.delavision.com/

Order Page

Ordering Details:
Please send a money order for £6.25 ($9.99), plus shipping, to
Gallerie de la Nougerede, 28 Cannon Place, Brighton BN1 2FB UK

Shipping charges:
If you are within the UK, please add £1.50
If you are within the EU, please add $2.00
If you are elsewhere, please add $3.50

Your book will be shipped by first class post if within the UK, or by Swiftair if elsewhere. You can expect delivery within approximately three working days from the day we receive your money order.

On completion of this order page, a confirmation page will appear, giving you your order number.

Please print this order page, and the confirmation page, for your records.

Thank you for your order, I hope you enjoy your book.

Home

Contact Us

To Order

Name:

Postal Address:

Email Address:

Number of copies wanted: (please include shipping per book)

Privacy Policy

Submit

[Home] [Contact Us] [To Order]

THE CONTACT PAGE

● Invite people to contact you and make it easy for them to do so. Larger organizations tend to regard customer feedback as an irritant, but receiving the views, needs, and opinions of both potential and actual customers for a new, small operation might make the difference between success and failure.

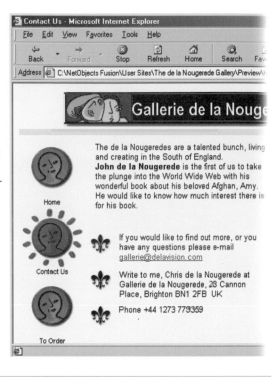

WEBSITE TIPS

● Keep your site updated on a regular basis.

● Consider qualifying for a third-party seal of approval from a credible organization such as BBBOnLine.

● If you want to generate more traffic to your website, link it to other sites and have them link to you. Also, remember to include your site's URL on letterheads and invoices.

● If you're dealing in objects other than books, the best purchase you can make as a seller is a digital camera because few people will even consider purchasing an item without a picture of it.

● Use the first page of your site to explain what is on your site and what people will find there.

● Place the navigation buttons within easy reach.

● Make your contact information easy to find.

● Use small display images to grab people's attention.

● Create some characters, if appropriate, and bring them to life.

JOINING A WEBRING

● A webring is a collection of websites that concentrate on a single theme and are linked together with a simple navigation bar. Each site features a banner at the foot of the screen that provides links to other sites in the ring.

● If you have your own website to market your goods, a webring can connect you to people interested in that topic, and to ones who are directed in their search to your site.

● The first step is to find a ring you'd like to join. Try looking at RingWorld: The

WebRing Directory (**http://www.webring.org/ringworld/**).

● There are several ways to find a ring that is relevant to you. One method is to enter the terms of your area of interest in the search field of this site and then click on **Search**.

WebRing - Microsoft Internet Explorer

File Edit View Favorites Tools Help

Back Forward Stop Refresh Home Search Favorites History Mail Print

Address http://dir.webring.yahoo.com/rw

Welcome to Yahoo! WebRing

Current WebRing User

If you joined WebRing before September 1, 2000,

Sign in here!

WebRing News

Yahoo WebRing New Features January 16, 2001 More...

Featured Rings

Wishes for the new year:
· peace in the Middle East
· an end to California's energy crisis
· a healthy mind, body, and spirit
· my very own aircraft cockpit

Link to other web sites like yours and...

● Increase traffic to your site!
● Use a simple navigation bar to link to other sites.
● Find concentrations of sites quickly and easily.
● Create a Ring and develop an online community.

Join a Ring

Join an existing Ring. Find the appropriate home for your the "Join Ring" links.

Create a Ring

Create your own Ring in 3 easy steps.

Find a Ring

Search or browse the Yahoo! WebRing directory below.

 afghan hound   Search

Done

Click here to begin the search ●

● Three matches are found, and then it's simply a matter of clicking on the ring that appears to match your needs most closely.

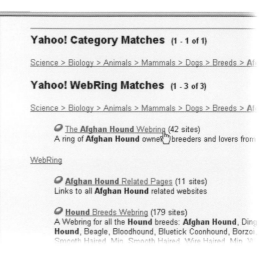

● If the webring appears to be the one that meets your needs, click on the **Join This Ring** button in the top right corner of the window. A form appears in which you can insert your URL, title, and description of your site.

● Each ring is maintained by an individual known as the Ringmaster, who determines the look and feel of the webring, and selects or rejects applications to join. You are informed of the Ring-master's decision by email.

USING SUBMIT IT! FOR YOUR SITE

● Rather than simply posting your site on the web and hoping that the major search engines will find and index it, you can register with **www. submitit.com** to connect your site with a large number of search engines and directories. You have to register your site, supply the title, description, and keywords, and contact information.

● Software analyzes your site by checking your meta tags, and advises on how you might improve them.

Your site is also checked for broken links and any spelling errors.

● You can send the information about your website to 40 search engines in less than one minute. All this is at a cost of just over $1.00 per week for two URLs.

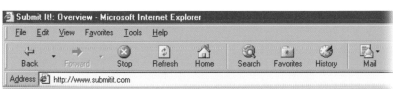

Overview
Pricing
Features & Benefits
Resources
Engine List
How it works
FAQ

Submit Itl: Overview

Get Listed on Search Engines and Directories

With the explosion of sites on the web, how can you make sure custome find you? SubmitIt! makes getting listed quick and easy! In just 3 short s you can get submitted to your choice of up to 400 search engines and directories. All for only $59 per year!

Why SubmitIt?

- Get listed in in your choice of <u>over 50 directories targeting specific locales</u>!
- Over 85% of web surfers use search engines to find what they ne
- Fill in your information just once and submit to the search engine and directories of your choice.

*Registering with **www.submitit.com** is a guaranteed means of promoting your website.*

SITE SEEING

Newly armed with the knowledge of how to buy online, you now need to know where to apply your skills. And if you're now tempted to sell online, here are some examples of how to do it.

INDEX OF WEBSITES

The websites listed here share one feature: they have all been available online at some time. Some are bigger and better stocked than others, but they all represent what a website can be. Inclusion does not imply endorsement. And don't forget the **www.**

1800flowers.com Send flowers anytime
1bookstreet.com Books on the web
800-trekker.com Science fiction store
999central.com Discount superstore

A

Adollhouseworkshop.com Complete line of dollhouse kits and furnishings
Aleather.com Leather ware and all your motorcycle accessories
Allbooks4less.com Bargain books
Allherb.com Herbs, natural health products, and remedies
Allpets.com Everything pets
Americanet.com Classified ads site
Art.com Art from artists, both the quick and the dead
Astrology.com Online horoscopes with instant delivery
Audiogon.com High-end audio gear
Autoaccessory.com Extensive range of automobile accessories
Avon.com Beauty products

B

Babystyle.com Baby accessories
Babysupercenter.com Further accessories for baby
Bargaindog.com Free personalized shopping service by email
Beadroom.com Antique and handmade glass beads
Bentleys.com Travel goods retailer
Beoutdoors.com Merchandise for outdoor pursuits
Bikeshop.com Bikes online
Biztravel.com Flights, etc.
Brainstorms.com Presents for children
Brooksbrothers.com The finest clothing
Brookstone.com Functional, distinctive, and unique consumer products
Bugleboy.com Clothes and accessories reduced on clearance
Burpee.com Beautiful gardens online
Buynsellit.com Collectibles that are off the beaten track
Buy.com The web's low-price general store

C

Ccvideo.com Classic films and DVDs

Cd universe.com Low-price CDs, videos, and games

Cellarexchange.com Wine and cellar site

Cigar.com Largest online selection of cigars and accessories

Classifieds2000.com Classified ads site

Clothingdirectories.com Directories of 100s of clothing stores

Coffeedirect.com Coffee shop

Collectorusa.com Buying and selling of rare coins

Crucial.com 56,000 memory upgrades

Curranscards.com Sports trading cards

Customgolf.com Customized golf clubs and equipment

Cvs.com Largest online pharmacy

Cyberrebate.com Hundreds of free products and free shipping

D

Dansgardenshop.com Gardening supplies

Decentexposures.com 100 percent cotton comfort designed by women

Deckthehouse.com All your decorating needs

Delias.com Outfits for women everywhere

Designer-bloopers.com Drapes and fabrics from mill overruns

Designeroutlet.com Overstock goods at reduced prices

Doodleville.com Cool clothes for kids

Drapers.com Ladies' fashions since 1927

E

Edelights.com High-end, gourmet gifts

Ediets.com Personalized diets

Ehobbies.com edeals for your hobby

Ejewelry.com Wide price-range of jewelry

Express.com More than just music, movies, and games

F

Finestkind.com Online store for fishing and tackle

Flooz.com Online gift currency that you send by email

Fossil.com Watches, sunglasses, and further accessories

Fragcity.com Fantasy, sci-fi, memorabilia, and a site worth watching

Fragrancenet.com Online perfumes

Freeclassifiedlinks.com Classified ads site

Freeclassifieds.com Classified ads site

Furnitureonline.com Home, school, and office furniture

G

Gardeners.com Every possible gardening need you could imagine

Giftexpress.com So you didn't know what to buy, huh?

Gigagolf.com Clubs and even computerized score cards

Golfsmith.com All that the golfer is likely to need

Gorp.com Books, maps, and videos to prepare the traveler

Greensprings.com Alternative natural health products

H

Hallmark.com Ecards supplied by the well-known Hallmark

Handspring.com Everything handheld containing a microchip

Harmony-central.com Merchandise of special interest to musicians

Helpingfoot.com Online shopping directory with a difference

Hersheysgifts.com Sweet gifts

Hickoryfarms.com Specialty foods and unique gifts

Hifi.com Audio and home entertainment

Homecraftshow.com Handcrafts from across the US

Humongous.com Entertaining software for children

IJK

Ice.com Jewelry and a range of other gifts

Illuminations.com Living by candlelight

Internetsoccer.com Connecting across the soccer world

Iparty.com Party planning and supplies

Jewelryweb.com Fine jewelry online

Kbkids.com Equip your kids

Kimon.com The site for finding great classic movies

L

Landsend.com Better outdoor apparel

Lang.com Calendars, cards, collectibles, and more

Levillage.com Very authentic French gourmet products

M

Magazineofthemonth.com A different discounted magazine delivered monthly

Magazines.com Subscribe to magazines at a discount

Mattressbroker.net If you can't sleep on it, it's not here

Merlite.com A unique jewelry range

Moret.com Workout gear for women

Musicyo.com Factory-priced brand-name musical instruments

Myartonline.com A person-to-person marketplace for art

N

Nationalgeographic.com The national institution's travel store

Newbargains.com Bright and cheerful discounted offers

Newyorkfirst.com It looks like a department store…

Nowdocs.com They print, bind, and deliver your documents

Nutrisystem.com Lose weight with online help and encouragement

O

Officefurniture.com Equip your home, school, and office with furniture

Officemax.com And now keep them in office supplies

Omniplayer.com Combine all audio formats into one player

Opticalsite.com Contact lenses, glasses, and sunglasses

Oriental.com The world's biggest toybox

Ourhouse.com Home and garden necessities and indulgences

Outletmall.com Discounted clothes with designer names

Outpost.com Almost everything electronic with free shipping

P

Paulfredrick.com Better men's clothing for every occasion

Peakhealth.net Starting with supplements and then everything else

Peggysnatural.com Health products, remedies, therapies, and more

Performancebike.com Bicycles, parts, and accessories online

Perfumania.com Aromas online and at low prices

Personalize.com Unique personalized gifts that they'll never guess

Postersast.com Decades of movie posters

Priceline.com Name your price and find an online taker

Prosportsmemorabilia.com Pro sports memorabilia, would you believe

R

Realbeertour.com The beers, the tour, and of course, the rewards

Realgoods.com Solar and eco living

Recordedbooks.com Unabridged books on cassette and CD

Riddell1.com Team equipment and more

Ritzcamera.com Photographic products and equipment

Ross-simons.com Bridal registry for all your wedding gifts

Royalcashmere.com The softest pashmina is available here

S

Sayitinstitches.com Customized embroidery for individuals and companies

Sharperimage.com Sharper gift ideas with added style

Signaturessuperstars Music merchandise for all music lovers

Simplydresses.com Prom dresses and cocktail dresses to die for

Smallflower.com Your body's ultimate user guide

Snowtraders.com Specialty snowboard equipment shop

Sparks.com Cards, gifts, and chocolates

Specialist-herbal.com Herbs for life

Spencergifts.com Gifts for those with a sense of humor

Stressless.com A resource for stress relief

Studentuniverse.com Travel with discounts if you're in college

Swissarmydepot.com More ideas than the knives have blades

T

Telplus.com Classified ads site

Tendollars.com Bargains, fun, and creative gifts at one price

Theadnet.com Classified ads site

Thebabyoutlet.com More accessories for the baby

Thecompanystore.com Linen and fabrics for the bedroom, the bathroom, and around the house

Thegolfwarehouse.com A golf superstore with news and tips

Thingsremembered.com Personalized gifts for any occasion

Tsisoccer.com Soccer footwear, apparel, and equipment

UV

Ubid.com One of the largest US auction sites

Underneath.com The source for online top-brand underwear

Usahotelguide.com 40,000 places to stay in the US

Varsitybooks.com Online discounted college books

W

Wicksend.com Candles, lamps, incense, and other bright ideas

Widerview.com High-end designer products for the home

Wine.com The world's wines, and advice on their selection

Wireacake.com For birthdays, anniversaries, and to say "I love you"

YZ

Yakpak.com Every kind of practical pack and bag you could wish for

Yardmart.com Your lawn will love you for visiting here

Youractivepet.com Adventure gear for your pet

Ziplinegolf.com Customized graphics to personalize your golf balls

GLOSSARY

BROWSER
See Web browser.

CERTIFICATE
In the context of web pages, a certificate is issued by a licensed certification authority and verifies the identity and ownership of a site.

DIRECTORY-BASED SITE
A website that groups its information, or the goods that it offers for sale, according to subject or type.

EMAIL (ELECTRONIC MAIL)
A system for sending messages between computers that are linked over a network.

GPS (GLOBAL POSITIONING SYSTEM) RECEIVER
A device that may or may not be handheld, which receives signals from at least three of the 24 GPS satellites orbiting the earth. The device measures the time each signal takes to reach it, and on that basis can calculate its position on earth.

HOME PAGE
The first page you see when you arrive at a website and typically contains a welcome message and hyperlinks to other pages.

HTTPS
The first part of the address of a secure web connection. The "s" stands for secure.

INTERNET
The network of interconnected computers that communicate using the TCP/IP protocol.

ISBN (INTERNATIONAL STANDARD BOOK NUMBER)
ISBNs are assigned to books and certain other publications by agencies in each country that operates the system. The numbers consist of 10 digits made up of four groups separated by hyphens.

NETWORK
A collection of computers that are linked together.

PROTOCOL
A set of rules that determines how computers communicate with each other.

SEARCH DIRECTORY
Database of website URLs and site descriptions organized by category and, in some cases, accompanied by reviews.

SEARCH ENGINE
Software that searches for specific information on the internet according to your search criteria. The term is commonly applied to websites that host search facilities.

SET (SECURE ELECTRONIC TRANSACTION)
By employing digital signatures that uniquely identify the sender of a request for an electronic transaction, SET enables vendors to verify that buyers are who they claim to be. Buyers are protected by their credit card number being transferred to the credit card issuer for verification and billing without the vendor being able to see the number.

SSL (SECURE SOCKETS LAYER)
A set of rules for two computers to communicate data that is encrypted and can only be read by those two computers.

UPC (UNIVERSAL PRODUCT CODE)
The UPC number is the 12-digit code that originally appeared on grocery items and which has spread to almost every retail item.

URL (UNIFORM RESOURCE LOCATOR)
An address on the internet. You type a URL into your browser address bar to visit a website.

WEB BROWSER
Software used to view websites. Internet Explorer and Netscape Navigator are two browsers.

WEB PAGE
A single page on a website that can contain text, images, sound, video, and other elements.

WEBSITE
A collection of web pages that are linked together in a "web."

WORLD WIDE WEB (WWW, W3, THE WEB)
The collection of websites on the internet.

WEBRING
Websites have banded together to form their sites into linked circles called webrings. Webrings are entirely open and free of charge to both visitors and members. Each ring is maintained by an individual known as the RingMaster.

INDEX

ACKNOWLEDGMENTS

PUBLISHER'S ACKNOWLEDGMENTS

Amazon.com, antiqueclassifiedad.com, Artists' Woods AutoTrader.com L.L.C., BBBOnLine, Inc., Ben Blumenfeld and George Reinhart of BidXS.com, Inc., CMI Services Inc., DealNetwork.com, ebay.com, eWanted.com Corporation, Half.com, Inc., HamQuest, Kwong Wong, Network Commerce Inc., Playle's Online Auctions QXL ricardo Plc, REI, SET Secure Electronic Transaction LLC, SportChalet, The Afghan Hound Webring, Tradenable, Trader Publishing Company, Verio Inc., Vladi Private IslandsGmbH, vrbid.com WeBeBeans, WINGS Online, Inc.

Microsoft Corporation for permisssion to reproduce screens from within Microsoft® Internet Explorer and Submitit.com.
Microsoft® is a registerd trademark of Microsoft Corporation in the United States and/or other countries.
Netscape Communicator software and website © 2000 Netscape Communications Corporation. Screenshots used with permission.
YAHOO! and the YAHOO! logo are trademarks of Yahoo! Inc.

Every effort has been made to trace the copyright holders.
The publisher apologizes for any unintentional omissions and would be pleased,
in such cases, to place an acknowledgment in future editions of this book.

All other images © Dorling Kindersley.
For further information see: www.dkimages.com